Dancing at the Chelsea

History as a Second Language

BAD ALCHEMY

BAD ALCHEMY

POEMS

Dionisio D. Martínez

W. W. NORTON & COMPANY · NEW YORK · LONDON

First published as a Norton paperback 1996

The text of this book is composed in Fairfield Medium
with the display set in Copperplate Gothic and Kuenstler Script
Composition and manufacturing by Maple-Vail Book Manufacturing Group.
Book design by Antonina Krass

Library of Congress Cataloging-in-Publication Data
Martínez, Dionisio D., 1956–
Bad alchemy : poems / Dionisio D. Martínez.
p.   cm.
I. Title.
PS3563.A733334B33   1995
811'.54—dc20   94-29262
ISBN 0-393-31531-2

W. W. Norton & Company, Inc., 500 Fifth Avenue, New York, N.Y. 10110
W. W. Norton & Company Ltd., 10 Coptic Street, London WC1A 1PU

1 2 3 4 5 6 7 8 9 0

For Mike Brooks

CONTENTS

ACKNOWLEDGMENTS

I'd like to thank the editors of the publications where the following poems, sometimes in earlier versions, have appeared or will appear:

Caliban: "Frank Lloyd Wright: The land," "Préludes"
Chelsea: "What the Men Talk About When the Women Leave the Room"
Confrontation: "Tableau," "Treason"
Denver Quarterly: "Kinescope," "Syllogism"
Georgia Review: "Simplicity"
Gettysburg Review: "Looking for Frank O'Hara on Fire Island"
Green Mountains Review: "Sometimes the Obvious Is a Blessing," "Temporary Losses"
Guadalupe Review: "Middle Men"
Indiana Review: "Burden," "Marcel Duchamp Descending a Staircase,"
    "Matisse: Blue Nude, 1952"
International Quarterly: "Valse-ballet"
Iowa Review: "Flood"
Michigan Quarterly Review: "Bad Alchemy"
Mid-American Review: "Gymnopédies," "Sarabandes," "The Vernacular of the Eyes"
Ploughshares: "Incomplete Combustion"
Prairie Schooner: "Gustav Klimt: The Kiss"
Seneca Review: "Avant-dernières pensées," "Gnossiennes," "Je te veux," "Nocturnes"
Virginia Quarterly Review: "Belated Valentine for Alina"
Witness: "Hysteria"

Walk on the Wild Side: Urban American Poetry Since 1975 (Nicholas Christopher, editor): "Fuego"

"Avant-dernières pensées" also appeared in *The Best American Poetry 1994* (A. R. Ammons, guest editor; David Lehman, series editor); "Fuego" in *Nebraska Humanities;* "Je te veux" in *Florida Suncoast Writers' Conference Anthology* (Gianna Russo, editor); "Matisse: Blue Nude, 1952" in *Museum Pieces* (Mark Irwin, editor).

The completion of this manuscript was made possible by a Whiting Foundation Writers' Award and a Hillsborough Country (FL) Arts Council Emerging Artist Grant. My thanks to everyone involved.

For their faith and support, I am deeply grateful to Linda Allardt, David Citino, Stephen Dunn, Rosie Fajardo, Judith Kitchen, Warren Hampton, David Lehman, Peter Meinke, Charles Simic, and Carol Houck Smith—my guardian angels.

The wheel is falling apart, but the revolution is intact.
—Henry Miller

ALTRUISM

I'd give you my seat, but I'm sitting here.
—Chico to Groucho Marx, in A *Night at the Opera*

Everything we know about death
is not enough to kill us. It's the last good season
of tourism and exile and I have a window seat
on the bus to the hotel. Beside me
is a man who refuses medical assistance,
claiming his god will intercede. They can't tell us
apart. That in itself is a considerable
blow to the gut of the revolution.
When they searched our bags, they missed
the huge shell I found half-buried in the sand.
At the hotel, I show it to the guard who
counts his paces on the other
side of the barbed wire. He's dying
without medical or divine intercession.
He mentions a wife, a daughter,
a garden with alternating rows
of lettuce and seashells. If the authorities
try to confiscate my shell, he suggests
that I tell them I'm dying.
Or dead, if I can get away with it. He points
to the bus parked outside, the dying man
waving from his window seat.
The guard says that if I bring the shell
to my ear, I can hear myself leaving again.

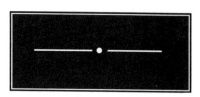

IN A DUPLEX NEAR THE
SAN ANDREAS FAULT

When she tells him about the lump in her breast,
he kisses her on the shoulder for the first time—a natural
reflex twenty-some years in the making. Suddenly,

their entire vocabulary revolves around *benign*
and *malignant*—words reserved
for these occasions—though they will say

very little now, then nothing for a long time. His hands
are just as pale and nearly as fragile as rice paper,
but she's not familiar with rice paper

and what she wants most desperately now
is a point of reference. Calla lilies bloom
like some glorious, abandoned music out on the lawn.

She takes one of his hands and thinks
of the spathe, which has the responsibility
of being leaf and petal, content and shape: without it

there would be no calla lily to remember,
nothing to see when she closes
her eyes and places his hand on her breast.

Where this train stops not even the engineer
knows: destination
is God's business and he tends to keep
things to himself.
Think of the Christ in Rio de Janeiro turning

his back
on the continent while he watches over the ocean:
from the foothills
even omnipotence seems limited and flawed. We
talk etymology, jargon,

how brief any word can be. When a smoker
in the metro
in Madrid wants a light, he taps you on the shoulder
and asks ¿Tienes
fuego? He wants to know if you have fire.

You've been studying
the underground routes, listening to the beautiful
percussion
of steel on steel, the trains leaving and the trains
coming and the late

trains making time between stations. Now and then
a wheel locked
and dragged along the track sets off a spark
and the spark disappears
in midair. From the Number 7 train—coming

out of the East River
and bound for Flushing—Manhattan is the open
palm of a long
severed hand, dusk a huge flame rising out of it.
The restless

boys from Queens are dreaming of arson at the 52nd
Street station. Let them
dream, let them flick their lighters as if they were
snapping their fingers,
let them be Romeos, let them be Jets for a day.

At the firehouse on 51st,
a man returning from a routine job takes off
his fireproof jacket
and walks away from the light. By the time he reaches
the street,

the man has become
invisible except for his t-shirt, which is almost
incandescent. A spark
climbs up the dark to the cigarette in his mouth,
the dark holds the fire's

tenuous glow in the caldron of its calloused hands.

SYLLOGISM

Wondering why the woman across the street is on fire
is a start.
The pyrotechnics of love are complex.

The boy who strikes a match on his mattress
during a nightmare
and the guilty husband who senses

flames on the tilted brim of his Stetson
and the girl in the burning raincoat
are not necessarily in love.

While still considered phenomena, these incidents
are fueled by the lesser emotions—
the more predictable outbursts, usually dislodged

from the creases of the soul and scattered
like severed molecules.
The woman across the street

was swallowed by a more stable substance.
When she joined the discussion, the argument
had been resolved.

You missed it by a day—the shuttle Atlantis
with its secret cargo looking for what's
left of the sky. It was my first sighting
of a night launch, the reds and greens like fallen

stars going home again. My entire block was out,
all of us shielding our eyes as if it were daytime.
One gets used to the days so easily here—
they seem to go on too long, then

vanish overnight. In no time, the fireball
was out of our lives. The neighbor with the best
view says the cape is practically across
the street if you measure the distance as the crow

flies, but all birds look the same to me,
and what do I know about flight?
I'm thinking *navigation* and how little the word
has to do with the sky.

Because the government has imposed a news blackout,
we must imagine the ghost crew navigating;
that is, sailing the rivers of the sky.
A friend recently told me that she noticed

how I've stopped talking about my father.
The day he died, I swore I saw him row
up a shallow river in the sky, a kind of secret
mission. You kept me on the phone for hours,

nearly convinced me that grief
is a town with two roads out. Maybe just
one if you spend the night with the bartender.
Oh, you and your cognac cures. It was always

you and your cognac—even on those nights
at the Chatterbox when the man
at the piano bar didn't show. Even after the money
ran out and the house on Cedar Avenue

began to fall, everything spilling out of our lives
like slow rivers of lightning in the sky.
What do I say now? Be careful with lightning?
I was doomed or blessed to love a woman who

understands the body too well. She tells me about
lightning, how electrical burns leave a mark
when they enter the body and a mark when they leave.
Everything between the two points—the whole crazy

path carved inside us—is instantly scorched.
Like the Midas touch in reverse, I start to think.
Then she tells me how a man, after being hit
by lightning, drove to the hospital calmly,

feeling absolutely no pain. She says he looked
so beautiful—the victim of a perfect
tan—as he walked into the emergency room.
The doctors knew. The doctors had seen

other bodies this beautiful, and they knew
the inevitable end of all beauty,
the bad alchemy that turns bronze to ash.
Once you're burned you're dead, she tells me.

The man didn't know it. He couldn't feel
his insides turning brittle at first.
Gradually, the tan began to harden, the body
began to figure out that it was dead.

One by one, the cells gave up. The doctors
explained the options to the man and to the man's
family, but only the man understood.
They could cut away all the dead tissue,

all the useless parts of the body.
But what would remain? the man wanted to know.
There would be a torso, maybe an arm,
definitely the shoulders and everything above them.

The man imagined himself literally half a man—
maybe much less—yet whole, and decided
he could live like that. You must know
how the will to live is a magnet and suddenly

north is anything that moves. You, with your love
for the fire that loves our bodies to death,
should know well. The man said yes, said
he'd go on regardless of the losses, which became

increasingly insignificant and real.
But while he slept, his family prayed for what
they thought was best, and everyone who had never
been burned nodded, winked, raised a thumb.

HYSTERIA

It only takes one night with the wind on its knees
to imagine Carl Sandburg unfolding
a map of Chicago, puzzled, then walking the wrong way.

The lines on his face are hard to read. I alternate
between the tv, where a plastic surgeon is claiming
that every facial expression causes wrinkles, and

the newspaper. I picture the surgeon reading the lines
on Sandburg's face, lines that would've made more sense
if the poet had been, say, a tree growing

in a wind orchard. Maybe he simply smiled too much.
I'm reading about the All-Star game, thinking
that maybe Sandburg saw the White Sox of 1919.

.   .   .

I love American newspapers, the way each section
is folded independently and believes it owns
the world. There's this brief item in the inter-

national pages: the Chinese government has posted
signs in Tiananmen Square, forbidding laughter.
I'm sure the plastic surgeon would approve, he'd say

the Chinese will look young much longer, their faces
unnaturally smooth, but what I see (although
no photograph accompanies the story) is laughter

bursting inside them. I go back to the sports section
and a closeup of a rookie in mid-swing, his face
keeping all the wrong emotions in check.

·   ·   ·

When I read I bite my lower lip, a habit
the plastic surgeon would probably call
cosmetic heresy because it accelerates the aging

process. I think of Carl Sandburg and the White Sox;
I think of wind in Tiananmen Square, how a country
deprived of laughter ages invisibly; I think

of the Great Walls of North America, each of them
a grip on some outfield like a rookie's hands
around a bat when the wind is against him; I bite

my lower lip again; I want to learn
to think in American, to believe that a headline
is a fact and all stories are suspect.

is the simplest form of architecture" and America
needs a simple house. Home should be
anything built by hand from the ground up, anything
that leaves dirt under your fingernails, anything light enough
to float above your life, but it's 1953 and your family
is building a bomb shelter in the yard. Frank Lloyd Wright
is being interviewed on television, where the world
is still black and white. You want him to give you
the dimensions of your life although you're still
too young and inarticulate to say it. All you can do
is fix your eyes on the man's hands. They are gesturing,
building something out of air, in the air. You drop
the shovel and the survival kit. Even your imaginary
weapons disappear as you try to put his hands into words.

Dear Larry: Looks like I won't need to borrow
the car after all: the trip to L.A.
is out of the question. I didn't know
a life could break down like a chemical.
Salt. Plutonium. The odorless noose
of carbon monoxide.
Up North a few years back, a group of kids
committed mass suicide in a 13-car garage.
You don't need plutonium to break down
the salt of life that keeps you in orbit.
When I worked at the medical library
I collected data on the 13-car garage story.
It was no longer a phenomenon.
Who needs plutonium? And the other 12
cars—what were they good for?
The quiet neighbor, who put up a wall
and a bay window where his garage door
used to be, has a cat's liver: nine
lives in that sucker.
The car sits outside now, and the man sits
on the hood. Who needs a garage?
His beers don't go down slowly, like sunsets,
but from here I can make it look that way.
Who needs carbon monoxide?
Frank Lloyd Wright came up with the solution:
the carport, a safe (i.e., doorless) garage.
One end of the roof of my carport
rests on the small utility room where I keep
my new lawnmower. I am proud
of the anonymity the mower brings me,
the way the noise of the 3.5 horsepower

engine and the action of the 22-inch blades
make me an instant member of the club.
Like some ritual humming, all the mowers
and edgers and weed trimmers
roll out of the carports, garages, tool sheds.
I start my engine. A little smoke
comes out, reminds me that I may still be
alive thanks to Frank Lloyd Wright.
The smoke dissipates. I wave,
no, I *salute* my neighbors, and go on.
My new 22-inch blades take to the grass
like a silenced man, when freed, to language.
Your letter arrived while I was buying
the mower. It didn't take me long,
when I came home, to run to the mailbox
and back, to put down the mail
and forget it. Life was too good. Why
would I want the possibility
of bad news from Ann Arbor, Seattle, Miami?
Trouble is, Larry, we're all scheduled
for a chemical breakdown sooner or later.
Here it is, your letter began,
the night before leaving for five
weeks in L.A.
And there were poems and newspaper
clippings (more ammunition
for the weapons we share) and mention
of a certain moment in the big city.
Your empty house is waiting for this reply.
Your mailbox is calling your name.
And we both live unfashionably
far from the cities on the edges. New
York, New York: you say it
once for those who knew all along
what you were going to say,

and say it a second time for those
who haven't been listening from the start.
You give them a litany of landmarks:
Times Square, Lincoln Center,
someone selling stolen watches from a
salmon-colored blanket on St. Marks Place.
Manhattan is larger than life when you
take it out of context.
I will say, instead, something discreet: L.A.
You abbreviate it to dispense with it
as quickly as possible, knowing all along
that no one is listening.
I will start the litany of the humble:
La Brea, Cinerama, Dodger
Stadium, the Capitol Records tower.
Out of context, they all sit
like angels on the head of a pin, their legs
dangling from the edge. I believe
in humility and a life at the end of each day.
I finish the lawn, look at my neighbors'
lawns and think, *Yes, yes, of course.*
I shower off the smell of oil
and gasoline and freshly cut grass.
I know the price I pay to live here.
I hold the face of God in my hands
and register no complaints. Who needs
a life of prayer against plutonium?
What good would it do?
A woman I had not expected to see again
stopped by last Sunday and spent the night.
With some sarcasm, I explained
to a friend the following day that the local
weather this time of year—hurricane
season—is analogous
to an intermittent affair: it rains,

it stops raining, it rains again,
and all along the sky
is easily identified by that consistent
shade of gray that holds it up.
There is always a constant in the midst
of nuances. Carbon monoxide
is the product of incomplete combustion,
a life unfinished, a voice
too soft to trust burning in the pale
blue flame of a long absence.
Thinking about it now, many hours later,
I find no humor in my remark,
no sarcasm. I find no solace in the weather
or in the face of God, that plutonium face
whose half-life begins beyond eternity.
I think of the first time someone
thought of eternity: it was a beginning,
a stillness only possible
after the body shudders out of control.
During one of the more infamous California
earthquakes, I lived in the duplex
on Lexington Drive, in Glendale.
After the house returned to its foundation,
I walked out to look for
cracks in the street. The reel in my head
played the Cinerama version of
a tremor and its aftermath: I would walk out
only to be swallowed by the open pavement.
But I walked out instead to the eerie,
inarticulate stillness of 7 A.M., people
in their bathrobes and underwear
along the sidewalks, our eyes
on the pavement's reassurance: no cracks,
no demonic fissures, no Second Coming.
Ironically, it was decades later

in Florida—where so many had gone, escaping
the faults out West—that the earth finally
opened, taking the highway and a row
of houses from Winter Park.
Just as the newsworthy dust was settling,
a house disappeared in Frostproof.
The sinkhole that claimed it began to fill
with rain, the way one might picture
Noah's grave if history had jumped the track
and caught him by surprise.
It didn't take long for the curious to arrive.
At first it was the locals, on foot
and understandably worried. They were followed
by a trickling of cars with increasingly
remote license plates. A harmless ride
around the hole, then northbound on SR 27
to places where life, in spite
of its uncertainties, seemed to walk
on relatively firm ground.
Now these busloads of pilgrims,
as if one could bottle up and take home
the faith that named the town.

KINESCOPE

Johnny Guitar is watching Duncan Renaldo.
Roy Orbison
is growing out of Elvis like a new
limb or that extra syllable every other
word acquires in the South.

What happens when you run into yourself?
You burrow deeper
and deeper until the center
is all there is, until going further
defeats the purpose of going.

You quiver inside yourself, your hands
gripping the spine, your eyes amazed
at the thin frame that sustains everything.
This is your own center of gravity.
This is the man you have become.

My father watches Duncan Renaldo. Duncan
Renaldo watches the moon in the sound studio.
He thinks the sky owes him a living. As if
living were something we did outside the body.
My father knows better.

We know what happens when two mirrors
face each other. I want to know
what happens when they stand back to back.
What kind of annihilation,
what self-devouring hunger for nothing.

NEED

The things you need to live, the people
you love to death—what would you call them tonight

if your life depended on the truth? Let's say a man
breaks into your house, holds

a knife to your throat and makes you call
your wife by her proper name. Suppose you call out

another woman's name. By now all the names
have become one: hers. But you don't know

if you'd be this confident with a knife so close
that the light bouncing off the blade

makes you squint. The Eskimo who shields
his eyes from the sun rising on his white-

on-white world has no all-encompassing word
for snow; instead, he names

each kind of snow as if it bore no relation
to all the other kinds. My father never called

my mother by her name. He even avoided
terms of endearment, fearing that they would gradually

take the place of that name. Calling her his love
would have torn all those ambiguous bonds that make

love remotely possible. My father would start to talk,
assuming that my mother knew she was being addressed.

SIMPLICITY

"Due to complications," according
to the preliminary findings. Due

—the doctor told us in his rehearsed
solemnity, the family gathered around him,

his head pausing in front of each
of us, his eyes meeting ours—

"to not-totally-unforeseen complications."
And so my father's death was at last

a fact with a label. And the old absolutism
remained incontestable: no one

ever dies from simplicity.

                • • •

No one has been overwhelmed
by the plainness of a life unquestioned.

Elsewhere and maybe a decade earlier
this poem would've been a shorter, simpler

thing, a mere description,
a scene being set like a table. The medium

would have been the message
and the messenger, the end

would have dragged its own means,
the poem would have questioned

nothing, and the death—my father's—
would have been briefly grieved,

our handkerchiefs going through the motions
not unlike the doctor, whose soliloquy

on complications was nothing but a new
character in Genesis 11—

a man in a white coat climbing the tower,
talking to himself a kind of medical Esperanto,

and no one close enough to overhear.

· · ·

My mother the seamstress had a seamstress
of her own, like the cook who will not

eat her own recipes: nearly everything we wore
was a product of my mother's sewing,

but she made nothing for herself.
Her seamstress, whose nickname begins

with a consonant for which there are only
approximate sounds in English,

made the dress my mother wore out of Cuba,
then again and again in exile as we unfolded

our maps of dead-end streets
and studied dictionaries filled with

the new country's euphemisms for *no* and *why*.

· · ·

No one, I'm willing to bet, has ever died
from hearing *no,* and the possibility

of being fatally wounded by a well-aimed
why as it ricochets from its intended victim

seems remote. My mother unfolded
the patterns carefully, like maps of the body's

surface—Simplicity, Vogue—all the way
from North America, where the body was something

for which we had no accurate translation.

· · ·

Dança general de la muerte, a fifteenth-century anonymous manuscript
from Spain, contains a series of simple patterns. Various medieval
characters speak to Death. And Death, in each case, has the last
word. The exchanges, bearing the tone of the doctor's voice outside
the room where my father was getting used to his deathbed, follow a
stifling symmetry and end with Death addressing "all those others it
has not mentioned here," leaving the imagination no room, making
sure everyone has a custom-made death, a pattern that cannot be
duplicated. Everyone deserves this much. It is, after all, fifteenth-
century Europe, and death is in vogue. In 1520, an altered version of
the *Dança* appears in Sevilla. Its penultimate section, comprised of
two stanzas, is an "advice," a recapitulation—a sign perhaps that his-
tory, if it teaches us anything, teaches us to leave less and less to the
imagination. The gist of it: repent though your fate is already dancing
toward you across the empty hall. My father's body eventually slipped
into itself, clung to the bed, and waited for whatever follows fate.
Simplicity patterns? Easier

· · ·

dance steps? Watching my mother cut her patterns
and lay them across the fabric, I thought

I would see clear through the bodies that would
wear what she was about to make. I thought

that if I knew the secret of the seams,
of the measurements, of the small

adjustments made just before the final
product is assembled, the garments would become

invisible. And maybe if I wore them—if I slipped
my arms into the sleeves the way my father's

body slipped, twenty-some years later,
into itself—I would become briefly

invisible to Death, and Death
would forget to teach me the little jig devised

to make me trip, eventually, over my own foot.

BURDEN

There is a code by which you live, unknowingly,
and just before the flesh completely
swallows the scar, you take a stand of sorts.

My father's death was followed by the coldest
winter of the decade.
My mother thought that the mere act

of dressing for the season was an unforgivable
display of infidelity, that comfort
is a weakness of those who are happy, and happiness

is the language of another season in another country.
All year, the hibiscus leans away from the oak
like a woman who walks out with an umbrella

and realizes, when the rain comes, that she wanted
to get drenched all along.
My father and the hibiscus gave in to the same forces,

but only the hibiscus made it back.
It was spring in every sense of the cliché. The row
of pines by my father's grave

soaked up the rain like music. My mother became
obsessed with language, with the idea
that in another country her words would have mattered

and perhaps my father would have had the resilience
of the red hibiscus.
She was learning to stand up to the elements.

Before my father, she finally admits, there was a boy
who stood across the street with a letter in
one hand and a flower in the other. There was one

who came to the door. One who followed her for blocks,
saying nothing.
They've all begun to reappear. Unchanged

and punctual as seasons, awkwardly wrapped bunches of
red hibiscus in their hands. According to my mother,
they all come with the same unimaginative story:

just happened to be in the neighborhood.
And they would stay, she says, if she would only
take that burden of flowers from their hands.

Now that I know where circus children
go when they run away, I have no desire to move.
I load the moving van and tell the driver
to go until he runs out of road or out of gas or
out of towns that refuse his worthless cargo.

To define what remains, we speak the language of
the invisible man who argues with the doctors long
after the amputation, tells them
that he still walks with a phantom limb. Literally.

I begin to count the change in my pocket
and think of Thoreau living on 27 cents a week,
walking too much, becoming accustomed
to the calluses from the ax, the strained
muscles and all that winter rising from the pond.

When I lay the change on the floor I find
a penny rubbed since 1944 by fingers not unlike
my own. I rub it too. For luck,
I think. All my superstitions are hand-me-downs.
What do I know about luck? What do I care if
the face of Lincoln rubs off on my fingers?

The oldest train route on the island began
a block from home. We laid coins
on the tracks and moved out of the way quickly,
remembering the kid who'd been half blinded.
I still wonder if a man with a glass eye
sees half of everything—half of the road, half

of the woman who will not tell him all the truth,
always a half moon regardless of the tides.

You want me to believe in everything, but there's
something to be said for knowing that a house
is not the world, that we can live without
the wicker furniture that made our house as tangible
as a father's arms. After all, sooner
or later they'll stop calling us orphans.

I hold my life savings in this hand.
No matter where I go, I carry foreign currency.

ED SULLIVAN AND THE DECLINE OF THE VARIETY SHOW

The first Sunday after it was canceled,
my mother wondered why.
The day he heard Ed Sullivan had died,
my Celtic father,
who already considered himself as American
as our neighbors,
blamed all the ills of society on the cancellation
of the Sunday-night
tradition. He said Sullivan would've lived
much longer
if the show had gone on. It was like those
couples that grow
into a single being after half a century
of marriage
and suddenly one half dies, and soon afterwards
is rejoined by the other.
My mother just wondered why the network
didn't renew the contract
till Sullivan died. Whatever my parents said
and thought, they seemed
to agree: this was blasphemy, this was a temple
desecrated
by vandals, and why wasn't it the end
of the world?
Someone had carved a hole at the core
of Sunday night.
Each week we would grow a bit more reluctant to
sleep
and Mondays would seem progressively distant.
In California, rumors
began to circulate. Doomsday prophets suddenly

had a license
to stand at the corner of Brand and Lexington,
in Glendale, at four,
four thirty, five in the afternoon, holding
out a hand, hoping
that God would take it the way, in cliff-
hangers, someone
always takes the hand of the character slipping
off the edge
and headed for certain death, the sea
below crashing
against the smooth rocks of the coast.
Maybe living near
the coast saved us, and saved our Sundays,
though I don't remember
the hand that pulled us up, and I don't
remember
who replaced Ed Sullivan, or how I learned
to sleep in peace
again. I was learning, in those days,
to count
on my fingers in French, and to say
the names of
cities I would mispronounce again many
years later
on the train to Paris. I had two languages,
but neither one
was enough to catch a stranger's attention.
I had expected
other things and somehow had managed to keep
France at a distance.
The first Sunday without Ed Sullivan, I sat
at my desk, my back
to the tv, and practiced my French—the alphabet,

the numbers, the names
of cities, the shape of the border that kept
the names
from falling off the edge and scattering
throughout Europe
when Europe was still defined by cartographers.

AFTERNOONS
WITH SATIE

PRÉLUDES

1

He makes you wait.
He proposes a language where waiting
for the next word means as much
as any word. You weigh
his seemingly insignificant and harmless
proposition against no proposition at all.

This is language as crude manipulation:
you have no choice in the matter.
It is language as game, he says.
The object is to decipher the world
during the capricious intervals that know
no rules of grammar.

It's not so much the sounds moving
toward and away from each other, he says,
as the silences that tremble
like beads of water on a slightly
uneven and unsteady surface,
the silences that stretch and recede.

This is not language, you tell him.
All along, he says, he knew you would say
just that.

2

The illusion of movement is a figure
standing still with so much conviction
that anything but stillness seems possible.

The possibility of illusion is a movement
of which only convictions are left
standing like a shuddering stillness.

The moving figure takes a stand in spite
of the receding stillness,
in spite of its own convictions. Possibly

he has figured out the extent
of the stillness, its trajectory, the degree
to which an illusion can stand on its own,

the only possible move a vague figure
can make once it's cornered and its eyes
are filled with peripheral convictions.

GYMNOPÉDIES

1

In a history of closed doors, an open
window means everything.
Even when I sleep past noon, I simply rub
this recurring dream of windows
from my eyes and resume the business of
living with so much still unnamed.
In the dream, the windows open onto other
windows. Finally, the need
for a landscape beyond them wakes us.
Today I opened all the windows of this world,
knowing that the wind would color in
all the missing details of the landscape.
This is scenery—this draft
through my house, this occasional
word from another house,
this brief sigh.

2

For nine years I dreamed I could walk on water.
Each night I returned to the same dream,
the same body of water.
My bare feet moved across an invisible
surface just above the surface of the water.
When the sea turned a near black
and the waves cupped themselves as if
hungry for me, the invisible surface
rose in proportion to the storm.
I was always safe in that weather.
One day the house of my dreams was empty

and locked for good. When they sealed
the front door, it was an accusation
and a mark of heresy I never understood.
I was on the street. That night
I did not dream. The following night
I dreamed of an empty house.
I never walked on water again.

3

They are building bridges across an endless
river. Brown skyscrapers
follow it, forming a more solid outline.
Birds fly the mad course of what has
become an object of desire.
Your city has claimed the river. You
have claimed the water of the city's
river. The buildings have claimed
the banks of your river.
The bridges reach out like claws and claim
nothing. The river has a natural
mistrust for bridges, for anything that
has no desire to possess.
The bridges wonder where they went wrong.
In my dream, they are building
the last bridge across the endless river.
In the eyes of a dream,
even an endless river is a finite line.

GNOSSIENNES

1

He went to China for a cup of tea.
Or he merely borrowed a pinch
of salt from the woman next door.
At this point everything was true.
Or to put it more accurately: everything
was possible.
Truth would come later.
Truth had never been an essential element
in his life. All accounts
of the past were made up of possibilities.
Truth was always a possibility.

2

The purpose of land is to break
the monotony of oceans. The purpose
of islands is to break the monotony
of continents that surface in the midst
of too many oceans.
The purpose of so much water is not clear.

3

There has always been this tendency
to scream on the way out.
Instead, there are small footsteps,
carefully measured breaths. It takes
an entire life to time an exit this well.
Even the future is considered:
Will the door shut itself behind him,

making the noise he has tried to avoid.
Will the door burst open before his
hand reaches the knob and the whole delicate
process begins.

To want is to desire. One who desires, however, is not necessarily one who wants. This is the logic of the heart. Romance languages will argue that wanting may imply love to some degree. Desire, they will tell you, knows its place and takes no risks. If a man is banished from a country of desire, he acquires an accent that is always foreign. He becomes susceptible to distances. Wherever he goes, vague references to love fall in his path. He will learn to say *I want* in many languages, always with an accent that even he will find alien. Desire will step gracefully out of the picture, leaving no words for the voice in the man's heart. And until the absence of desire is the only thing left to grasp, he will not know that a man with an accent is marked for life.

Let's consider the problem of perspective. The
theater has yet to solve this matter. The props

have been carefully arranged so that the Greek
ruins grow smaller and the floor descends as the

scene stretches away from the audience. This way
the actor exiting appears to be swallowed by dis-

tance. The problem begins when the actor and the
ruins can go no further. Here the illusion loses

its power. The actor is still too tall to appear
distant. The scene is one of a terribly perplexed

giant. The audience feels embarrassed for the ac-
tor. The actor swears he will not return to the

stage. This is fear: a man with no place to go, a
conflict he can't possibly resolve, a helpless and

rather unsympathetic audience. Except for those in
the mezzanine, whose unique perspective never

allows them the luxury of illusion. Their applause
is not in honor of magic. This is where the actor

looks at the end of each curtain call.

At the office party last night, half of us were
strangers to almost everyone. We were there as

escorts for the other half—the company's nucleus.
Such status is conducive to the luxury of inven-

tion. I thought I could carry a tune. The others
followed. Surprisingly, the music managed to com-

pose itself after fits and starts like someone in
front of a long mirror after a good hard cry. I

changed my name for the occasion. It was like
changing suits: from gray to a darker gray. Extrav-

agance, whose voice memorizes phrases composed
exclusively of subtle words, is the only thing

eloquent enough to rise above the chatter of strangers.

SARABANDES

Our prayer, therefore, ought to be short and pure, unless it happens
to be prolonged by an inspiration of divine grace.
—from St. Benedict's Rule for Monasteries

1

Ordinarily, persistence is a virtue.
But this is not an ordinary sky, and ours
is not an ordinary thirst. Our times

call for rain. Our prayers, our long
walks to the nearly empty well—everything
we do is a note in a chant for rain. Polyphony

is not, as we thought at first, the soul's
affliction. It's a product of too much prayer,
a blade of voices piercing the silent blue.

2

The attributes of sin speak for themselves.
Their stories are necessary. A simple
equation will justify them all. Prayer

is the cosmetic equivalent of salvation;
its bottles of soothing ointments empty them-
selves on our blemished lips. This candle

is as brief as the prayer on my lips.
My faith is as lethal as the candle's flame.
The flame is as delicate as my faith in prayer.

3

I know what I saw. It was, at best, an uneasy
compromise, the leveling of the landscape
as mere token. We still remembered a promise of

miracles. The ratio of prayers to miracles
has not diminished the hope we carry as the only
real legacy. Each day we scatter

prayers across the flat land that surrounds us.
If nothing rises, there's always more land,
there are more prayers, there's a legacy at stake.

IDYLLE

In today's mail I found the chain letter you've been sending for years. I know your handwriting, your desperation, the peculiar way in which you fold the paper. This plea, you tell me, has been around the world three, maybe four times. This plea is sacred. This plea is our last hope for anything. In theory, intimidation can penetrate anything. We all break sooner or later. The letters are carefully packed with case histories that go off like timed explosives. I can see you waiting for each one to go off, wondering if the one you designed for me will do the trick. One summer, you say, a Portuguese fisherman received this letter and burned it. He spent the rest of his life trying to read the ashes.

AUBADE

I thought it over. This letter is not sacred. It promises nothing. It is a plea for anything, which is like saying a plea for nothing. There was a faint barking as I walked toward the window. It was the sound dogs make when a stranger approaches. I began to doubt my own presence in the house, my hands opening the window to more barking. You must copy the entire letter, you said. The copies you make, the warning continued, must be indistinguishable from the source. I made the copies. I slept with the words beside me. This morning I thought it over. I tore the letter, replaced it with a blank sheet, folded the sheet in that peculiar way I learned from you.

MÉDITATION

On the coast of Portugal they began a tradition, you say. With the letters still inside the sealed envelopes, the wives of fishermen burn the mail they receive. This way, you tell me, superstition is impossible. But isn't this a superstition of sorts? It's really a mockery of belief, you say. I sometimes wonder how we've managed to correspond this long through chain letters. I wonder how we've been able to sustain this dialogue between two anonymous voices. I think of the widows along the Portuguese coast, their chain mail used as fuel for their stoves. I think of them selling rotten cod fish wrapped in anonymous letters that have circled the world three, maybe four times. I am spending the night in Viana do Castelo. I will send this postcard unsigned.

NOCTURNES

1

He closed the deal on the night. A real
bargain, he said. And the city was reduced
to a room, the man's constant body in bed,
the sheets glowing like phosphorus.
One flaw in the design made it possible
for an occasional body to slip in.
The sheets would glow a bit more brightly
in its presence. Each time it left, the body
would leave more of itself behind,
until there was no absence to speak of.
The man began to count on the occasional body
and its lingering presence, which he now calls
memory. He understands that the laws
of necessity draw their own conclusions.

2

Even night is a product of residual light.
What they call absolute darkness is the art
of knowing how to lower the shades almost
completely, knowing exactly how much is enough.
We measure the varying degrees of shadow
in the residue. We know that a shadow
is the object from which it is cast.
We are beginning to understand the principle.
Night, we have finally admitted,
cannot extend beyond the things it evokes.
The concept of night as entity is impossible.
The varying degrees of light in each shadow
speak for the silence between the stars.

3

I apologize for my dialogues with the light.
I apologize for the voices in the red hibiscus.
I apologize for the small details still
discernible in the sparse grass of the yard.
I apologize for the birds that would not nest
in the absent dark of the tree,
for the long evenings, and the square
of sun on the bark of the tree, and the promise
that prevented the last hours.
I apologize for the leaves moving
like carbon copies of leaves across your face.

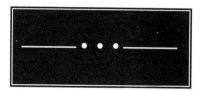

YEARS OF HOPE

What my 1731 Stradivarius cannot play, my ears will invent.

My catalogue of inventions is worthless in the absence of desire.

I came for the music, but I stayed for you.

My tenuous landscape is nothing but layer upon layer of paper.

I sleep on the faultline and dream of being swallowed. At 5:19 in the morning one bird and then another will wake me.

What good is the dark without music?

You are as punctual as winter light.

Years of Solitude

To the one who sets a second place at the table anyway.

To the one at the back of the empty bus.

To the ones who name each piece of stained glass projected on a white wall.

To anyone convinced that a monologue is a conversation with the past.

To the one who loses with the deck he marked.

To those who are destined to inherit the meek.

To us.

YEARS OF RECONCILIATION

The mime troupe is in town again. They want to reconstruct us bit by bit.

This is where the house went up in flames.

This is how we walked away, trying to salvage nothing.

That's us, building our separate houses in the aftermath.

There were ashes to be swept away, years of debris, pages and pages of unresolved music.

Here we are, looking out of our respective windows at the space between us.

Of all the illusions, forgetting is the most dangerous.

YEARS OF FORTUNE

Suppose we count backwards and nothing happens.

The palm reader says I live on intuition.

Something tells me you're home for good, your unpacked bags
nothing to worry about.

This morning I paid off the mortgage. By the middle of the
afternoon I noticed that the house had not changed.

Indiscriminate wishes determine the length of a season and the
falling of the light around here.

Escape has such a final ring to it. Let's just say we're
taking our time in returning.

For better or for worse, ours is a variant of a rather common
story.

Years of Judgment

One lethargic word crawls out of your reach and confronts you.

Each breath unfolds with intentions of its own.

Even the slightest preoccupation with absolute stillness is a significant increment of time.

Everything is measurable.

Salvation is a deliberate leap into the eye of a cataclysm.

Believe like a man and you will drown in a drop of faith.

Believe in nothing and the first rains will level your house.

Years of Vision

In a matter of minutes I destroyed the journal I had kept for
15 years, maybe longer.

A man in love soon learns to be unfaithful to himself.

I changed my name and taught myself not to answer when you
called me by the old familiar one.

It became obvious that accidents are worth repeating.

Each day I woke a little closer to the sea with little more
than my cobalt blue history to keep me afloat.

I bought a shirt to match the earth of each new country I
stumbled into—*terra cotta, terra firma, terra incognita.*

In countries with nothing but overabundance, language has the
luxury of moving backward—*red hibiscus, dark leaves.*

Y E A R S   O F   D I S C O U R S E

are not always preceded by years of silence. More than likely,
they follow unfulfilled demands.

An arsenal of threats is dismantled.

The hands of the adversary begin to look surprisingly life-
like.

For the agnostics, a man with cancer in his throat heals
himself and begins to sing like a broken angel.

Those most susceptible to nostalgia are reminded of the
mythical Age of Miracles.

An arsenal of memories, long abandoned, is discovered and
restored.

Familiar voices reappear. In proportion to the sky, they are
whispers.

SOMETIMES THE OBVIOUS
IS A BLESSING

They came looking for a fossil of us.
With time, they assumed, we would have fused
into a single bone, indecipherable as our names.

The deeper they dug, the more their own hands
turned into fossils.
Blueprints of our names would only take them

so far. Perhaps you can't get here from there.
Perhaps they should look beneath their own houses,
tear out the floors methodically,

number and stack every tile, crawl
down calling their own names until the answer
stops coming back. God knows what artifacts

they would bring out,
what broken testaments of our beliefs.
Without a code, what value would these things

have for them?
What false names would they assign to each find?
Even when I knew I was losing you,

I was comforted by the knowledge that no one
would speak like this again.
No two people would ever call each other

by these names. But my maps were worn, love.
Every road was a geological accident,
a path naturally carved between mountains.

When we finally agreed on a common language,
maps had been updated and a new road
paved over each of our carefully chosen words.

One by one, love, our words went silent;
the traffic of silence filled the fresh pavement,
traveling mostly in our direction.

Now it's down to this dust through the sifter.
Only slightly deterred by their failure,
the archaeologists dig even deeper to forget us.

REENACTMENTS

Cinéma vérité, she says, as if that
were enough to convince us.

• • •

The girl at the car rental agency has that Jean Harlow
look about her. On my way to Kentucky at two
in the morning I begin to drive backward through time,
my future dissolving in the rearview mirror.

• • •

She changes her name to protect her innocence.

• • •

At the novelty store someone is buying a poster of
Patty Hearst playing Tanya: armed with the look
of someone whose weapon is loaded. Behind her, a cobra
is about to strike. Resemblances between Tanya
and the reptile have gone unnoticed, unexamined.
When the customer begins to roll up the poster,
the cashier says, "I saw that movie too."

• • •

She believes in degrees of perfection—
with each successive frame the subject
is closer and larger yet somehow less defined.

• • •

A revival house in Buenos Aires is showing *Blow Up*
to an audience consisting solely of Julio Cortázar,
who has been dead for years and sits in the front
row, wringing his hands in frustration: he has trouble

picking up and connecting the clues.
It appears he's distracted by a premonition.

• • •

*Art imitates art, she says. It's the nature
of things.*

TREASON

Parachutes
were still made of silk.
Scarves fell

through a careless sky,
so many scarves
dragged

across Europe while the Glenn
Miller Orchestra
played nothing but "Perfidia."

When the troops opened
their rip
cords, the fields that would

break their fall
waited with anticipation
and second

thoughts,
like women who worry
that the neck

can't feel
the difference
between the silk

of a new scarf
and the hands of a tender
strangler.

TABLEAU

He came home with a primitive vengeance.
It was almost beautiful.
Life as he'd known it here didn't

stand a chance. The tv
was the first thing to go. He raised it
like a heavy chalice. For a moment

the tableau seemed unbreakable, the veins
in his arms frozen blue.
The family watched as if he were

a child about to take his first step.
No one flinched when the tv
finally hit the terrazzo and the fragments

sprayed the room. Later that evening,
when everything had been swept away, they
all followed him out of awe, or was it fear?

Probably fear, they think now,
their conclusions about him drawn at last.
He could sit for hours at the window,

his open shirt like a lace curtain waiting
for wind. This much they remember about him.
He seems so far away now.

It was this remoteness that saved him from
himself. He knows that. Wherever
he is. Whatever he's done with the thought

of having come home to a country that
had grown in his absence. Or a country
that had not changed but merely

found its way into his new eyes.
The box labeled *memorabilia* was empty.
The few surviving relatives could not remember

where the others had gone, which
ones had died over the years, which ones
were still around but somewhat less visible.

MOTO PERPETUO

1

I've been walking in circles for what seems like days.
They've been playing Paganini, but you know

how intermittent the conscious ear
can be. How selective. Walking has nothing to do

with distance as clearly as Paganini
has nothing to do with the violin that plays him hard.

2

How it hurt Jackson Pollock, during his black
and white period, to hear the critics say

that he was painting black *on* white; how important
the gaps and absences were to him;

how crucial the distances, the gulfs; how
critical each emptiness to each composition.

3

There is that moment in, say, the finale of Beethoven's
Fifth, when you hear nothing between the various

false endings, so you make your own music,
a bridge of silence from one illusion

to the next. A deeper and more refined
ear—Beethoven's ear—takes care of this.

MATISSE:
BLUE NUDE, 1952

I fail to cut your hands
in proportion to your head,
your bowed head in proportion
to your breasts, your
breasts in proportion to one
another though only
the left one is visible from
this angle.
Where did I put the missing
hand, the eyes,
the small blue
breath of what you will say
when you see yourself naked
and begin
to speak to the unrecognizable
blue of your form? You will wait
for an answer from what
you think is a stranger.
Why do I talk about strangers
when I should be talking about
the recalcitrance of my hands,
how my fingers
curl up and refuse to follow
the images I have in mind for them?
I keep seeing the two strangers,
nothing but the sound of blue
in what they call breaking the ice:
one speaks, the other pretends
to listen. I cut a blue
path into your heart because love
is more manageable than paper.

LOOKING FOR FRANK O'HARA
ON FIRE ISLAND

Some stunned animal
waits in the middle of the road,
its gaze tangled
in the oncoming headlights.
Does it think it's seeing love at last?
I know better and am tempted
to avoid it, but my temptation
is not that strong.
I kill to feed the little
gods of sorrow.
This must be what they mean
when they warn us that
we're all potential criminals
or potential victims.
Every call on the police radio
makes suspects of us all,
our names waiting
like no-shows on the guest list,
the party canceled,
the finger sandwiches and the music
ruined, the night ruined,
bottles and stacks of plastic cups
on the wet bar,
everything you can imagine
delicately ruined,
ruined, and the host
and the hostess sitting
at the shallow end of the pool,
their bare feet
provoking the still water.

MARCEL DUCHAMP DESCENDING A STAIRCASE

Like water. The bucket
      in the well

is too deep for you to know
      if it's carrying

water, to see if it's full.
      You judge

by the weight of the rope,
      the voice

of the pulley. An educated
      guess. Like picturing

a crossword puzzle in your head.
      The clues. The empty

boxes. The essential
      other—the one

who comes to fill
      the puzzle. A steady

pencil in his hand
      like a confident voice.

        • • •

A man crossing the street
      hears voices. He lies down

very deliberately
        on the pavement

and writhes
        until the voices

tell him to move on.
        Hours after he clears

the intersection,
        traffic

is still backed up for blocks:
        no one wants to make

the first decisive move.
        Traffic like water

in your hands. Voices
        in the well.

• • •

When two innocent men
        confess to an imaginary

crime, making it suddenly
        real, the president

reluctantly opens
        his crime reduction package.

It's full of nothing but
        streetlamps. An extra

light for every block
in your neighborhood.

This is why tonight
you will shed a long shadow.

. . .

Though the city
has crumbled beyond recognition,

you feel some comfort
when tourists are encouraged

to pick it up with their teeth.
There's a good chance

that the finished product
will look nothing

like its blueprint. Reconstruction is off
to a slow start. One brick

at a time. Like water.
Like the weight

of the rope in your hands. The pulley
with a voice thick as traffic.

. . .

The freeway system, obviously modeled
after a crossword puzzle,

doesn't know its limits. A road
will become a coil, intersecting

itself many times. Though you know
        there's no water in the well,

you will drink from the bucket.
        One morning, an elevated span

of road resolutely
        falls on itself. Like a word

erased from the puzzle. The right
        word eludes

the indispensable *other,*
        for whom each road

is defined by its vanishing
        point.

Winter's why we talk about silence,
why we spend too many nights
awake, rehearsing how we will say
that everything about this devastatingly
unoriginal ceremony has been said.
The trick is how to say it.
Or how not to say it. Or how to walk
casually to the door, leaving the keys
on the table in the living room
on the way out.
Winter's why we leave. Silence is
why we keep coming back to pick up
something that was left
behind because it was left unsaid.
Winter is why the skin beneath my skin
is another man who knows
he is leaving, and knows a woman
the way he knows distance.
The skin you know
is like an old quilt—every patch and
every seam where one would expect it.
The other skin is less predictable,
perhaps a bit more fragile.
The weakness of our flesh is why we
run into winter. Head on.
Ultimately we can only trust our doubts.
I wrap this heavy quilt around us.
I say what I think you want to believe—
that beneath this skin
there is no other skin, inside this
man nothing but silence and the faith

with which we must believe
in a silence we've come to know by what
we've heard.
I beg you to close your eyes
and trust me, and hope that you don't.

THE CULTIVATION OF ORCHIDS

This boy with the eyes of an owl
will not grow wings.
Instead, a man who lives on air will grow
inside him. In time, many arms
will sprout from the boy's
body, which knows how to adapt
from one life to the next. When the man
grows too large for the space he occupies

and the boy starts to ache and complain,
the man will learn to twist one foot, bend
his knees just so, relax the neck
until his head comes down and rests
between the shoulders.
With the man correctly positioned, the boy

can lie down, his skin draped tightly
over his rib cage, and we will not notice
this other life inside him.
He will need all his arms to carry
himself, to keep the two lives from coming
in contact with one another.
In time, the boy will outgrow the man.
His arms, having become unobtrusive

and ordinary, will welcome
the sleeves of heavy coats.
His eyes will look progressively smaller.
The man will give himself a voice
and a name. The boy will begin to hold

his breath and eavesdrop
on conversations between the man
and the woman who has come
to draw him out.

MIDDLE MEN

With Lorenzo the Magnificent dead,
Michelangelo wonders
what will become of the Medici.
There are rumors.
The body beneath his firm hands
is turning into flesh.
He traces the shape of a new
world across her back.
He rests his hands and feels
her entire body breathing
slowly into the pillow.

What does it take?
He imagines the men who preceded him.
The man who taught
the woman beneath his hands
how to breathe like this, and the man
who shaped her small breasts,
and the man who brought her here.
He imagines them all dead.
He's seventeen, believes in eternity
and thinks he knows
the shape of God

                  • • •

although at this point that shape
is only a frightened Christ,
crawling back from death
like a crab out of the sand.

The Medici are crumbling like sand.
Christ did not die for them,
or for this body beneath the hands
that will turn
stone into virgins

and madonnas. Michelangelo
is seventeen
and believes in nothing but the voices
of God at odds with one another
in the heart of the marble.

. . .

King João II turns Columbus down.
Portugal has dreams of its own:
its cartographers have burrowed
their way to the Spice Islands,
making the merchants of
Venice feel the ache of obsolescence.
Venice itself is almost irrelevant.

. . .

For the record: Columbus shares favorable
sailing conditions with the last
Jews—expelled from Spain
the day before the three caravels
head for the new world.

. . .

If it's true that the words on top
of the painting by Sebastiano del Piombo
were added after the death
of Columbus, and this
is really the portrait of a nobleman . . .
If this is true,

. . .

anything is true.

When Juan Rodríguez Bermejo shouts
¡*Tierra!* he hasn't sighted land.
He's remembering
an afternoon when he was seventeen
and saw
for the first time a woman—much
older and perhaps a little
closer to God—breathe

into a pillow
like God himself breathing life
into a stone.

WHAT THE MEN TALK
ABOUT WHEN THE
WOMEN LEAVE THE ROOM

STIEGLITZ

The room itself. The women. The absence of women
in the room. What the absence of women does
to a room. The sound of all those women getting

up and leaving; all of them at once, like wild
birds or hunger. How the world can be conquered
if only . . . Just don't tell the women.

What the absence of women will do to men
eventually. Fears. Men talk about fears, bad
dreams, women leaving, the room swelling with

the absence of women. Bad dreams have a way
of walking in the room when the women leave.
Each dream is an afterimage of a woman leaving.

Scott Fitzgerald

Last night he was talking about living with
a woman in Paris. He was talking about rain.
He said he didn't mind the weather, just

the inevitable talk that makes it happen.
We noticed it was raining. It had been raining
for days, he said. He was talking

about life in Paris after a good rain—how the bums
fall like bad weather or bad news, how they line
the sidewalks, and sleep wrapped in the steam

that rises from the city beneath the city.
He was thinking of moving underground.
He was telling us how the metro

closes at ten in Madrid, at midnight in Paris.
He was saying it as if it made a difference,
as if saying it would change the schedules

the way it seems to change the weather.
He was talking about sleep—how he slept
in Europe when it rained too much,

his bad sleep in small rooms, imaginary sleep.
He was talking about the pain of living with
a woman who talks to the dead in her sleep.

Offshore, the expanding light of dawn is saying nothing again.
My eyes, when I rub them like this, say they want to see stars.
I'm waking in Brockport to the smell of late
breakfast and a somewhat overdue spring. This pantheist land
says it will forgive itself again, it will bloom and forget
and sweep the breezes back into Lake Ontario.
The lake says yes. The other lakes, the smaller ones
just south of here, have that feel of Monet gone sepia, those
fragile impostors that want to pass for water lilies. They say little
and they say it softly and you have to listen
very carefully for words you will need tomorrow, the names
of villages, alibis too small to remember.

I wake alone in the house where you once sat for hours
facing a late sun and afraid to complain. I didn't notice that your eyes
were saying enough of this, pull down the shade.
My superstitious neighbor with the green thumb says today
is the only day to prune whatever has survived the near-
frost of the South. I leave my garden bare, especially
the unruly hibiscus that clutched the bars on the living room window.
I've cut it down below my knees and the window says
look, that's her face against the glass, the light in her eyes again,
but when I go inside, it's only the window, it's only dust
and unanswered mail on the sill, it's only the light.
I say nothing or I say your name and I hear
the light complaining that it can't get enough of itself,
I hear the slow dissolve of the light, it's so predictable. I held you
here once, or I imagine how I would've held you here. This
is the light and this is your body which is solid light
and this is almost all I remember.

I wake on the floor, face down, with your name in my hands.
The warm Spanish tile says listen. A telephone
rings and I wake holding the receiver and it's your name I hear
over the line, so for all practical purposes I wake with your name
in my hands. It's someone from the hotel staff asking you
to put me on the phone, asking us to pay, to leave,
to stay home, to make our own beds, to climb
down the fire escape, to elope, to wake in a country
with a name neither one of us can pronounce, to buy land,
to sell everything. We will always
be tourists to the hotel staff. The telephone says
it's not time and it's not over and it's not so late.
I bring out my scrapbook, it's full of pressed leaves, leaves
from every tree that has sheltered me. There are sounds
at the door, or variations of a single sound,
a kind of tapping like a dog or a very small child
who taps accidentally, who doesn't really want to come in.
Something taps and says it's time. I am wearing
the chain with the little broken watch that is a symbol
of nothing in particular. The gears are partially
exposed, like mechanical fossils.

I wake in airplanes, in a train station near the Pyrenees,
I wake in my own arms, like this, and like this,
I wake in the theater, you are with me, your sister is sitting
behind us, it's early, it's always early, isn't it, it's Saturday
and we are listening to the only music we can afford to love.
I wake in the high desert of California, I wake in Atlantic City,
I wake while walking down 12th Avenue towards Flagler.
When I wake, I'm halfway there, wondering
why not somewhere else. I wake though I'm already awake.
It's a life of waking constantly, even in my sleep. I wake
in San Antonio, where the poplar is not a tree and it's in ruins

and it says your name and it remembers a time
when I would've stolen a yellow bicycle and a handful
of wildflowers for you, a time when I would've gathered
enough thread to mend all the broken moons in the galaxy.

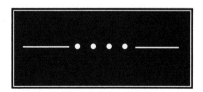

THE VERNACULAR OF THE EYES

1

For many, this landscape is only snow falling on fallen
snow. When you say *Dr. Zhivago,* it's mid-

summer, nineteen-sixty-something again,
and on the black and white tv in my living room a man

is walking through the woods. Seeing is just a matter
of discipline. You point to the lake: your wife

salvaged most of the dock after the last northeaster.
Now the boards, stacked behind your house, wait

for the weather to say it's time to rebuild.
We go to where the old printing press

is working again. Leaflets, announcements, unbound
books. Stacks of harmless language with the occasional

slightly uneven letter that was part and parcel
of the aesthetics of the times. I've traveled thirty-

seven years to say this, to mold out of snow
the single careless word that will take me home.

2

The man on Fifth Avenue has sorted his vintage
magazines by date. He knows what voyeurs

we are: he has heard us talking about the insignificance
of pain from a distance, how calmly we watch

the betrayal of Playa Girón, the Prague Spring blooming,
the fall of Saigon, the surrender

of the Japanese, all those vicarious wings we grow
each time Amelia Earhart soars out of our sight.

3

An old man sells newspapers outside my father's store.
I'm seven years old, maybe younger, when I ask him

about the large, blank squares on nearly every
page. On windy days, I watch

the newspapers—made lighter by all that missing
print—struggling like so many useless wings

beneath a handful of stones. The old man mentions
the law and how some words

are better kept inside, like a sickness. (Think
of the child who, when given a blank sheet of paper

and instructed to draw anything, simply
writes across the bottom of the sheet: *Children*

playing in a blizzard.) At home, my father makes
coffee for my mother and for himself.

Each morning, our ration grows smaller. My father
waits for the water to boil and stares

at the missing text of the newspaper on the table.
Many still refer to these days as *the triumph*

of the Revolution. All I remember is too little coffee.

NOTES & DEDICATIONS

"Fuego" is for Jonathan Aaron.

"Bad Alchemy" is for Gayle Natale (1944–1990).

"Hysteria" is for Ana Menéndez.

The quote in "Frank Lloyd Wright: The land" is from FLW's book *The Future of Architecture* (Horizon Press, 1953).

"Incomplete Combustion" is for Laurence Goldstein.

"Temporary Losses" is for my sister, María M. Menéndez.

The poems in the sequence "Afternoons with Satie" use the titles of piano compositions by Erik Satie (1866–1925).

The sections of "Flood" are titled after some of Humberto Calzada's "water paintings," which triggered the poem.

"Sometimes the Obvious Is a Blessing" owes its title to Ricardo Pau-Llosa.

"Reenactments" is for Rosa Menéndez.

"The Cultivation of Orchids" is for Marisella Veiga.

The first section of "The Vernacular of the Eyes" is for Bruce Bennett; the last section is for Nancy Linsky.

Dionisio D. Martínez, born in Cuba in 1956, is the author of two previous collections of poetry—*History as a Second Language* (Ohio State, 1993), winner of the 1992 Ohio State University Press/*The Journal* Poetry Award, and *Dancing at the Chelsea* (State Street Press Chapbooks, 1992). He was the recipient, in 1993, of a Whiting Writers' Award, the *Mid-American Review* James Wright Poetry Prize, and a Hillsborough County (FL) Arts Council Emerging Artist Grant. Martínez's work has been widely published in journals and anthologies, including *American Poetry Review, Kenyon Review, Iowa Review, Denver Quarterly, Virginia Quarterly Review, Georgia Review,* and the 1992 and 1994 editions of *The Best American Poetry.* His book reviews frequently appear in the *Miami Herald,* the *St. Petersburg Times,* and elsewhere.

Following his family's exile from Cuba, in 1965, Martínez lived in northern Spain and southern California. A Tampa, Florida, resident since 1972, he is an affiliate writer at the University of Tampa and a collaborating artist with the YMCA National Writer's Voice Project.